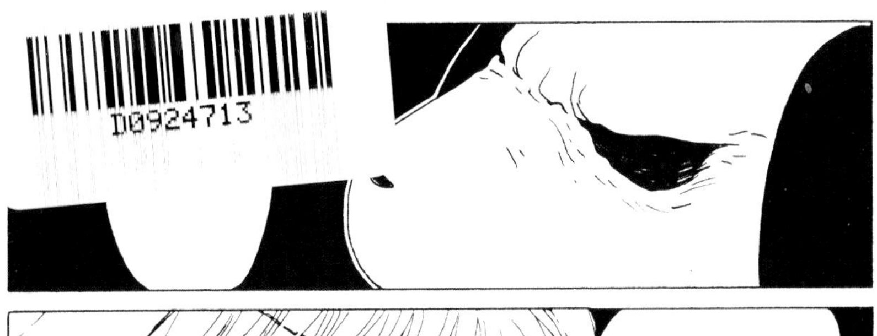

...SO IF YOU REALLY UNDERSTAND, THEN...

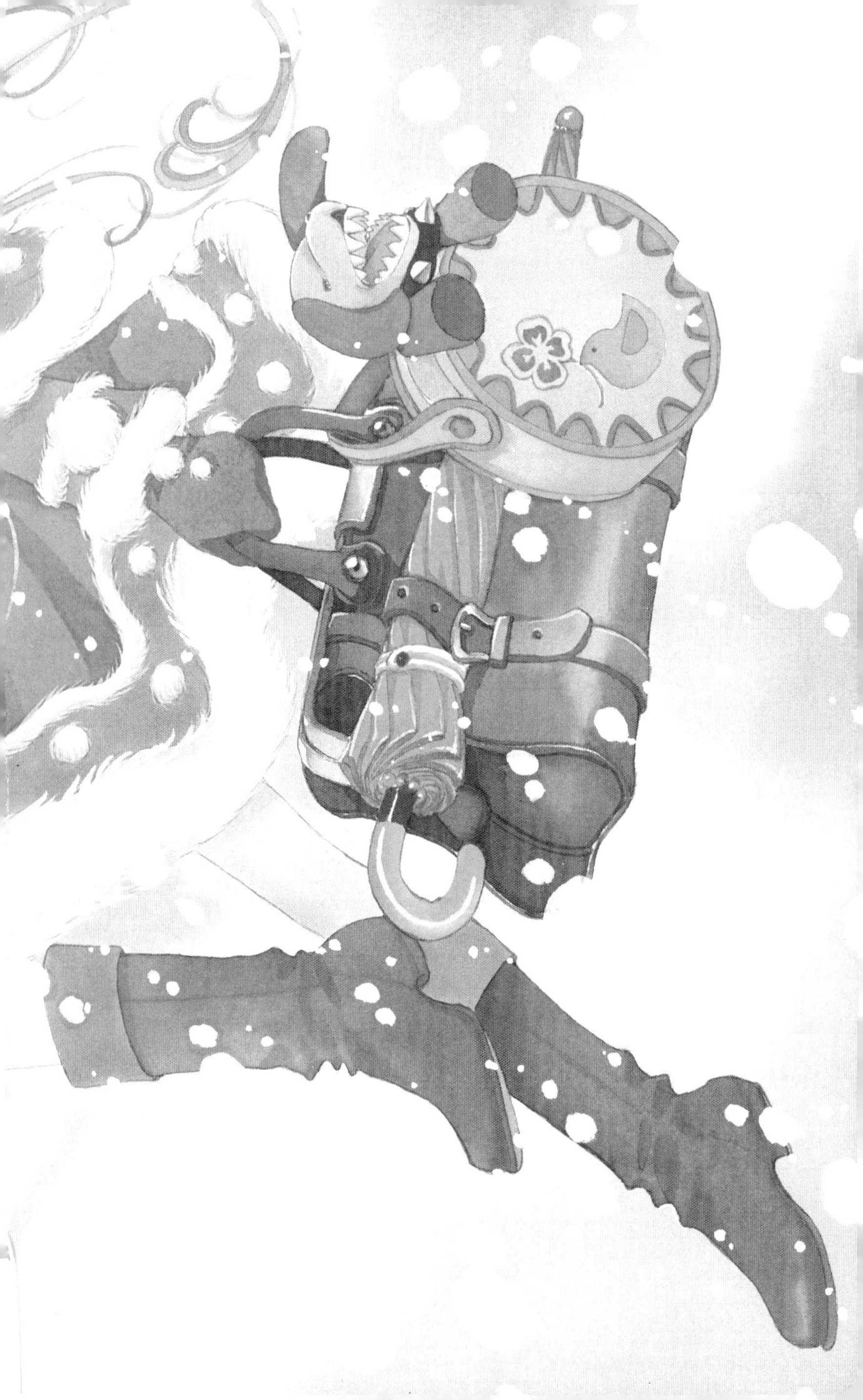

Kobato.
Ch. 1
The Very First Test
Presented by
CLAMP

...WHAT'S THE MEANING OF US BEING SQUISHED IN HERE SO EARLY IN THE MORNING!?
I FEEL LIKE THE FILLING IN A SUSHI ROLL!
BUT, YOU KNOW! FOR SOME REASON, MEETING IN A SECRET BASE LIKE THIS IS JUST SO...THRILLING! AND FUN!
KYUIIIN (VWEEE)
KYUIIIN
WHO SAID YOU COULD HAVE ANY FUUUN ?!!
KYAAAAAH!!
GOO (BLAST)

KOBATO HANATO!
BISHI (SNAP)
YES!
WHAT IS YOUR WISH?!
THERE IS A PLACE I WANT TO GO!
AND TO THAT END, WHAT DO YOU NEED?!
I MUST FILL UP A "BOTTLE" TO THE BRIM WITH WOUNDED HEARTS!
AND BEFORE YOU CAN DO THAT?!
I MUST DO MY BEST TO EARN THAT "BOTTLE"!

HOW WILL YOU EARN THAT "BOTTLE"?!
I MUST TAKE AN APTITUDE TEST TO SEE IF I AM CAPABLE OF LIVING HERE.
YES!
AND THAT TEST STARTS RIGHT NOW!
THIS ALL GETTING THROUGH THAT SKULL OF YOURS, HUUUH ?!
Y-YES, IT'S ALL IN HEEERE!
BIKU
BIKU (FLINCH)
SFX: GIRAAAN (GLEEEAM)
THE RESULTS OF THE TEST WILL BE DETERMINED BY THE EXTENT TO WHICH YOU CAN ACT ACCORDING TO THE COMMON-SENSE RULES OF THIS PLACE!
YES, SIR!

NOW!
GET TO IT, KOBATO!
DO WHAT EVERYONE WOULD EXPECT YOU TO DO IN A PARK IN THE EARLY MORNING!
GO ON THEN, GET'CHER BACKSIDE OUT THERE !!
DA (DASH)
YES, SIR!
GASA (RUSTLE)
GOSO (DIG)
GASA
GOSO
WELL, WHAT DO YOU THINK OF THIS, IORYOGI-SAN?!
WHAT, ARE YOU S'POSED TO BE SOME EXHAUSTED BUSINESSMAN CATCHING A FEW WINKS DURING LUNCH?!!
KYAAAAAH!!!
DOGOO (KABOOM)

ほて
HOTE
ほて
HOTE (TROT)

CAN'T YOU EVEN SPEND A LITTLE TIME IN THE PARK LIKE A NORMAL PERSON?!
I'M SORRYYY...

WAAAAH! I'M GOING TO MISS THE BUS!

UM... IS SOME-THING THE MATTER?

ARE YOU FROM THESE APARTMENTS?! SORRY, BUT PLEASE DO ME A FAVOR AND TAKE THIS TO THE TRASH AREA FOR ME!
EH? EH?!
PASU (TOSS)
ぽす

WAAAAH!

SO NOW IT'S MY RESPON-SIBILITY, HUH?

PERFECT! THE NEXT TEST BEGINS!
GIRARI (GLINT)

NOW YOU WILL SHOW ME...
...WHAT PEOPLE DO WITH TRASH!
Y—
YES, SIR!
SO THAT GENTLE-MAN ASKED ME TO TAKE THIS TO THE TRASH AREA.
TRASH AREA...
WHERE IS THE TRASH AREA?!
KYORO
KYORO (GLANCE)
きょろきょろ

SIGN: TRASH COLLECTION AREA / COMBUSTIBLES - TUESDAY + THURSDAY; NON-COMBUSTIBLES - MONDAY + FRIDAY; OVERSIZED TRASH - BY APPOINTMENT

SIGN: LET'S REDUCE THE AMOUNT OF TRASH WE THROW AWAY

カァァ
KAAA (CAW)
LOOK AT MISTER CROW AND ALL HIS FRIENDS...
THEY'RE AFTER THE TRASH.
IF YOU DON'T HURRY UP, THEY'LL PECK IT RIGHT OUTTA YOUR HANDS!
AFTER THE TRASH...
MISTER CROW AND HIS FRIENDS ARE...
...AFTER THE TRASH!
こみはなるべ
減らしましょ

BA (WHAP)
MISTER CROW!
PLEASE HELP YOURSELVES !!
GUHAH!
WHADDAYA THINK YER DOIIIIIING ?!!

YORORO
(WOBBLE)
ヨロロ...

WHAT MADE YOU THINK IT WAS A GOOD IDEA TO SIC THE CROWS ON US, HUUUH?!!
B-BUT...
MISTER CROW LIKES TRASH, AND THE SIGN SAID TO REDUCE THE AMOUNT OF TRASH, SO...
...BY GIVING IT TO MISTER CROW, THE AMOUNT OF TRASH WILL BE REDUCED, SO...

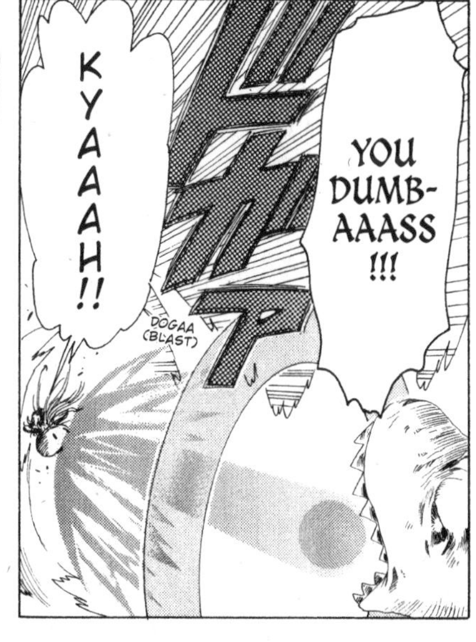
YOU DUMB-AAASS!!!
KYAAAAH!!
DOGAA
(BLAST)

YOU DON'T DESERVE THE NAME KOBATO ANYMORE!
WHAT AN AWFUL THING TO SAAAY!
"DOBATO" IS GOOD ENOUGH FOR THE LIKES OF YOU!
KOGE
(PUFF)
コゲ
KOGE
コゲ

UM... UM...
HOW AM I DOING ON THE TEST?!
SUCHA (SWISH)
PEKEEEE (SLAAASH)
DOBATO GETS ZERO POINTS!!
I'M GOING TO DO BETTER NEXT TIME!!
HEH!

Kobato.
Ch. 2
The Secrets of Nabe!?

TOBO
とぼ
TOBO (PLOD)
とぼ
TOBO
とぼ
FOR THE LOVE OF—! AREN'T THE WORDS "COMMON SENSE" WRITTEN ANYWHERE INSIDE YOUR HEAD?!
KOBATO HANATO!!
Y-YES, THEY ARE!

SEE? I CAN EVEN SPELL IT!
GURI (RUB)
GURI
OOMPH!

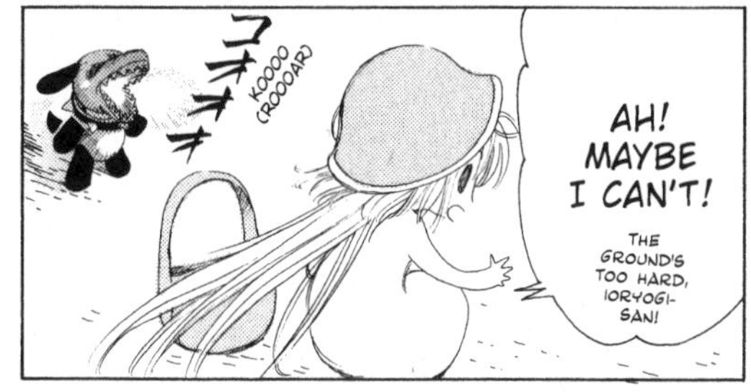
AH! MAYBE I CAN'T!
THE GROUND'S TOO HARD, IORYOGI-SAN!
KOOOO (ROOOAR)

KYAAAAH!!
GOOOOO (BLAAAST)

I'M NOT TALKING ABOUT WHETHER YOU CAN WRITE IT ON THE ASPHALT OR NOT! AND YOU MESSED UP THE STROKE ORDER ANYWAY! WHAT'S WRONG WITH YOU?!!!
LIKE, "POKE"!
BUT...LISTEN! IN THE MANGA I PICKED UP AND READ YESTERDAY, THE GUY JUST POINTED HIS FINGER LIKE THIS AND MADE HOLES IN WALLS AND STUFF!

SURE, MAYBE IF YOU WERE A MASTER OF THE HOKUTO SHINKEN MARTIAL ARTS, YOU COULD DO IT TOO!!
I'M SORRY-YYYY!

ORA (SNARL)
ORA
I'M SORRYYY!
PURURURURURURU (RRRRRRRRING)
PURURURU
HEEEY, FUJIMOTO! YOUR CELL PHONE'S RINGIIIING!
OH, SORRY.
WHAT'S UP, PART-TIME-KUN? IS IT YOUR GIIIIRL-FRIEND?
PURURURU
Yomogi Kinder-garten
IT'S THE KINDER-GARTEN.
COULD BE AN EMER-GENCY. GO ON AND ANSWER IT!

HELLO? FUJIMOTO SPEAKING.
SAYAKA-SENSEI?
EH?
THOSE CREEPS SHOWED UP THERE AGAIN...?
I'LL BE RIGHT BACK.
PI (BEEP)
I'M SORRY ABOUT THIS.
IF SOMETHIN' HAPPENED AT THE KINDER-GARTEN, YA BETTER GET GOIN'!
I REALLY AM SORRY FOR LEAVING YOU IN THE LURCH WITH ALL THESE CUSTOMERS.
SAYAKA-SENSEI'S IN TROUBLE. DON'T WORRY ABOUT ME!

THANK YOU VERY MUCH!
PEKO (BOW)
TA (DASH)
SFX: KUSUN (SNIFFLE) KUSUN
GAMI (GRIPE) GAMI
YOU REALLY DON'T HAVE A CLUE ABOUT COMMON SENSE IN THIS WORLD!
YEEES... I'M SORRY!

SFX: WAI (CHATTER) WAI
HA! HA! HA!
ADD A NABE TO OUR ORDER!
AH! THREE MORE BEERS OVER HERE!
ISN'T MY ODEN READY YET?
YEP! COMING RIGHT UUUP!!
WOOOW... HE LOOKS AWFULLY BUSY.

SAKE
THIS IS THE SEASON WHEN SOMETHING WARM GOES DOWN NICE, AFTER ALL!
SAKE DOES TOO, OF COURSE!
I'M SORRY, BUT WE'RE FULL UP FOR SEATS AT THE MOMENT!
EXCUSE ME! I'M NOT HERE AS A CUSTOMER.
I JUST NOTICED HOW BUSY YOU ARE, AND...
GOT THAT RIGHT! TODAY OF ALL DAYS, I HAD TO LET MY WAITER LEAVE ON SHORT NOTICE TO TAKE CARE OF SOME-THIN'!
KYUPISHI (ZIIING)
...IT'S A TEST!
HUH?

THIS VERY FOOD STAND ...
...IS WHERE WE ARE GOING TO TEST YOUR MEALTIME COMMON SENSE!
GIRAN (GLINT)
KIRAN (GLEAM)
Y—
YES, SIR!!
ORDER UP! MOTSUNABE FOR TWO!
FU-FU-FU-FU-FU... NOW SHOW ME HOW HARD YOU CAN WORK...
WAI わいわい WAI (CHATTER)
ISN'T MY ODEN READY YET?
BEER! BEER!
I LOOK FORWARD TO WORKING WITH YOU!!
OKAAAAY?!

TAKE THESE BEERS OVER THERE!
OKAAAY!
ANOTHER ORDER OF NABE HERE!
OKAAAY!
HANG ON!
WHO SAID YOU COULD TEMP AT A FOOD STAND?!
DOBATO-OOOOO!!

SORRY TO KEEP YOU WAITING!
OH! THANKS.
WOULD YOU MIND COOKING IT FOR US?

EH? Y-YOU MEAN ME?
YUP, IT'S ALL YOURS! THANKS!
AH HA HA!
SO LIKE I WAS SAYING...

SHOW ME YOUR STUFF!
I WANT TO SEE KOBATO'S MASTERY OF NABE!!
I-I'M SUPPOSED TO...
...COOK THE NABE ......?
HYAH!
ZARARARA (SPLOOOSH)
HEY! YOU CAN'T PUT THOSE IN BEFORE THE POT BOILS!
EEH?!
AH! YOU SHOULDN'T PUT THE MEAT IN FIRST!

EH?!
TOPU (BLUB)
TOPU
AAAAH! WHAT ARE YOU POURIN' MILK IN THE POT FOR?!
EH? BUT IT'S SO NUTRITIOUS!
NOW YOU'VE GOT CHOCOLATE?!
PEOPLE FEEL MORE ENERGETIC WHEN THEY EAT SOMETHING SWEET, THEY SAY!
WAAAH! NOT NATTOOO!
KYAAAAH!!
BOKO (GLUB)
BOKO
BOKO
PURU (TREMBLE)
PURU
WHY, YOU... IT'S LIKE SOMETHING OUT OF AN ARTIST'S RENDITION OF HELL...

FUEEEH ...
W-WELL, IT'D BE A SHAME TO WASTE FOOD, SO...
K-KO-BATO... THAT HURTS ...
ぎゅ
SFX: GYU (SQUEEZE)

KOBATO, STOPPP IIIT! CAN'T BREA...
AH!

IT'S GOOD!
FOR REAL?
SFX: MOGU (MUNCH) MOGU

AH! IT'S TRUE! THIS IS BETTER THAN I'D EVER HAVE EXPECTED!
もぐもぐ
THIS IS GREAT! IT REALLY IS!
YOU'RE RIGHT!
GOSH, IT REALLY IS TASTY!
THIS IS GOING ON MY REGULAR MENU!
YUM, YUM!

THANK YOU SO MUCH!!
どきどき
DOKI DOKI (BADUM)
KOBATO, TODAY...
...YOU GET ZERO POINTS FOR NABE COMMON SENSE.

EEH?!
SFX: SUCHA (SWISH)
スチャ
WELL, THAT SAID, THE NABE TURNED OUT TO BE GOOD IN THE END.
FORTY POINTS!
SHU (SWIPE)
AWWWW!
BUT... YOU KNOW WHAT?
KOBATO IS GOING TO TRY HER BEST TOMORROW TOO!
MAN, I FEEL LIKE EATING MORE OF THAT NABE!

Kobato.
Ch. 3
Kobato's Christmas

WOOOW! WOOOW!
YOU'RE AWFULLY MERRY TODAY, KOBATO.
OF COURSE, IT'S CHRIST-MAS!
IT'S DECEMBER 24TH, CHRISTMAS EVE, TO BE EXACT.
I KNOW ALL ABOUT THAT! IT'S THE DAY BEFORE THE REAL CHRISTMAS DAY, RIGHT?!

WELL... TECHNICALLY ACCURATE, BUT I WONDER...
KOBATO, DO YOU KNOW WHAT PEOPLE DO ON CHRISTMAS?
OF COURSE I DO!
GOOD!
THEN SHOW ME WHAT YOU'VE GOT!
DO THE THINGS THAT ARE APPROPRIATE FOR CHRISTMAS!
YES, SIR!!
WON'T YOU PLEASE SPEND THE NIGHT WITH ME IN A HOTEL?!
HUUH?!

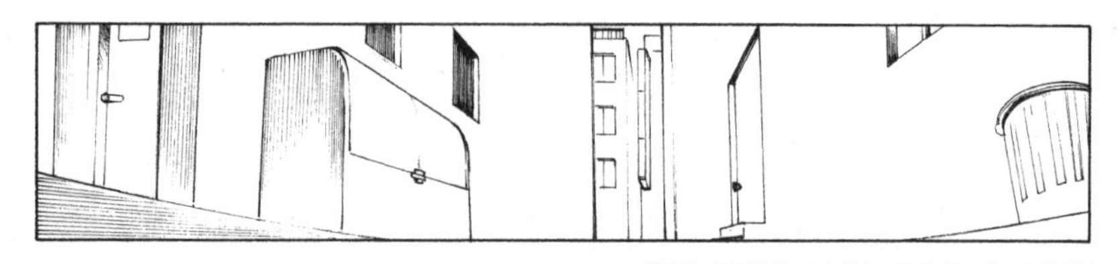

SIGN: ENOMOTO ELECTRONICS

I HEARD A VOICE.
BUT NOBODY WAS THERE!
IS SOMETHING THE MATTER?
MAYBE IT WAS JUST A KITTY?
NOW, WE HAVE TO HURRY HOME! PAPA BOUGHT US A CHRISTMAS CAKE AND IS WAITING FOR US!
OKAAAAY!!
CHRISTMAS CAKE!
CHRISTMAS CAN'T BE CHRISTMAS WITHOUT CHRISTMAS CAKE, CAN IT?!
WELL, I GUESS... BUT SAKE'S MORE ESSENTIAL, IF YOU ASK ME...
LET'S GO GET OURSELVES SOME CHRISTMAS CAKE!!!
WHOA!!

WOULD YOU CARE FOR A CHRISTMAS CAKE?
欧風菓子 チロル
SIGN: EUROPEAN BAKERY TIROL
WELL, YOU'RE ON THE RIGHT TRACK WITH THE CAKE FOR CHRISTMAS CONCEPT, I'LL GIVE YOU THAT...
THE OWNER OF THIS SHOP REALLY IS SUCH A NICE MAN, ISN'T HE?!
MAYBE HE'S NICE... OR MAYBE HE'S JUST GULLIBLE.
OHHHH... MAN, I THINK I'M FROZEN! A HOT DRINK WOULD SURE BE NICE ABOUT NOW...
THANK YOU VERY MUCH!
...BUT WHAT'S UP WITH YOU GETTING AHEAD OF YOURSELF AND AIMING FOR A PART-TIME GIG SELLING CAKES?
THIS STORE'S KINDA WEIRD TOO, LETTING A STRANGER TAKE A JOB, JUST LIKE THAT.
カラン
KARAN (TINKLE)
カラン
KARAN

THANK YOU SO MUCH FOR HELPING OUT IN THE COLD!
NOT AT ALL. THANK YOU!! THERE'S ONLY ONE CAKE LEFT!
HYOI (LIFT)
ヒョイ
HERE!
HUH?
PLEASE TAKE THIS CAKE AS PAYMENT FOR YOUR HELP.

THANK YOU SO MUCH!
WAH-WAH! THE CAKE!
PEKO (BOW)
AAHHH! I'M SORRY!
AH! YOU MIGHT NOT WANT TO SHAKE IT—
KYAAAH! I'M SORRYYY!!
...IS THIS A COMEDY ACT OR SOMETHING?

BOX: EUROPEAN BAKERY TIROL

GEEZ, JUST LOOK AT HOW LATE IT IS.
ALL 'COS OF THE SHOPKEEPER-DOBATO COMEDY ROUTINE.

CHRISTMAS CAKE ON CHRISTMAS...
WOULDN'T THIS BE... COMMON SENSE?
OOH... WELL... I GUESS IT COUNTS.
HOORAAAY!!

OH NO!

IS SOMETHING WRONG?
PATA (PATTER)
パタタタタ
TA
TA
TA
"TIROL" IS... ALREADY CLOSED...
GAKKURI (SLUMP)
がっくり

BY "TIROL," YOU MEAN THE BAKERY OVER THERE?

YES. I MADE A PROMISE TO MY SON THAT I'D DEFINITELY COME HOME WITH ONE OF THEIR CHRISTMAS CAKES, BUT I HAD TO WORK OVERTIME, AND NOW IT'S SO LATE...

UM... HERE!
EH?

IT'S A "TIROL" CAKE!
EEH?!

I HOPE IT MAKES HER SON HAPPY!
はっ
HA! (GASP)
BUT THAT MEANS OUR CAKE IS ALL GONE...
UMM ...
WHAT IS THAT YOU HAVE ON YOUR HEAD?

IT'S SANTA-SAN'S HAT.
AND ISN'T SANTA THE GUY WHO GIVES PEOPLE CHRISTMAS PRESENTS?

THEN—!
SUCHA (SWISH)
KOBATO EARNS NINETY POINTS!
90
FUWA (FLOAT)
THANK YOU SO MUCH!

AH!
SNOW, HUH?

MAY EVERYONE HAVE A VERY MERRY CHRISTMAS!
BUT IF IT'S SNOWING, WHERE'RE WE GONNA SLEEP?
AH!

Kobato.
Ch. 4
A Wonderful Otoshidama

IORYOGI-SAN.
UH-HUH.
SIGN: HAPPY NEW YEAR!
新年のご挨拶
TODAY IS THE FIRST OF JANUARY... NEW YEAR'S DAY, RIGHT?
UH-HUH.

EVEN THOUGH IT'S NEW YEAR'S DAY, IT'S REALLY QUIET, HUH?
NEW YEAR'S DAY IS A HOLIDAY, REMEMBER?
AND THIS IS A SHOPPING DISTRICT.
NEW YEAR'S DAY IS A HOLI-DAY...?
?
WELL, WHEN YOU WORK, YOU JUST FEEL LIKE A BREAK ON NEW YEAR'S.
SEE?
SIGN: EUROPEAN BAKERY TIROL
NOTICE: HAPPY NEW YEAR. WE WILL BE CLOSED FROM DECEMBER 30TH UNTIL JANUARY 3RD.
欧風菓子 チロル
THIS PLACE IS CLOSED TOO.
謹賀新年
12月30日より1月3日まで
お休みさせて頂きます。
欧風菓子
チロル

YOU'RE RIGHT.

SUTON (FWUMP)
NIKO (GRIN)
NIKO

WHAT'RE YOU JUST SITTING HERE FOR, KOBATO?!
WELL, SINCE YOU'RE SUPPOSED TO TAKE A HOLIDAY ON NEW YEAR'S...
...I THOUGHT I'D TAKE ONE UNTIL THE THIRD MYSELF!
KA (FLASH)

DON (BOOM)

WELL, I SUPPOSE THERE'S NOTHING WRONG WITH WANTING TO TAKE A VACATION OVER NEW YEAR'S...
...BUT NO VACATIONING ON SOMEONE ELSE'S STOREFRONT!
SHIKU SHIKU (SOB)
HOTE HOTE (PLOD)
I'M SORRY-YYY!
BUT I'M NOT REALLY SURE WHAT I SHOULD BE DOING DURING NEW YEAR'S...
SIGN: ENOMOTO ELECTRONICS / WE WILL BE CLOSED UNTIL JAN. 5TH.
I CAN'T WATCH TV SINCE THE ELECTRONICS STORE IS CLOSED, AND...
OH MYYY.
...NO NEW BOOKS AND MAGAZINES ARE OUT FOR ME TO READ...
OH MYYY.
THAT'S 'COS PERIODICALS PUBLISH THEIR NEW YEAR'S INFO IN THE PREVIOUS ISSUE.

BUT...
...SINCE THE STREETS ARE DESERTED, TESTING YOU WILL BE TOUGH TOO, KOBATO.
OH, PLEASE! PLEASE FIND A TEST FOR ME TO DO!
I REALLY WOULD LIKE MY "BOTTLE" AS SOON AS POS-SIBLE!
IT WILL NEVER DO IF I DON'T START...
...FILLING IT UP TO THE BRIM WITH WOUNDED HEARTS.

......YOU GOT THAT RIGHT.
'COS YOU WANNA GO THERE, DON'TCHA?
OH!
FIRST TOWNS-PERSON SIGHTED!
PERFECT TIMING! GO HELP HER!
EH?!
UH...UM... IS THERE ANYTHING I CAN HELP YOU WITH?

WELL, I'LL BE! WHAT A LOVELY YOUNG LADY!
AND WHAT MIGHT YOUR NAME BE?
I'M KOBATO HANATO!
WELL, THEN. SHALL WE GET STARTED RIGHT AWAY?
THANK YOU VERY MUCH!
WOULD YOU TAKE THIS DISPLAY OUTSIDE MY FRONT GATE FOR ME AT ONCE?
YES, MA'AM!!
GU (PULL)
GUKI (CRACK)
FUGYU?!
AH. THE SOUND OF DISASTER.

SFX: PIKU (TWITCH) PIKU

BESIDES, THERE'S STILL SO MUCH MORE I'LL NEED YOUR HELP WITH!

OKAY!!

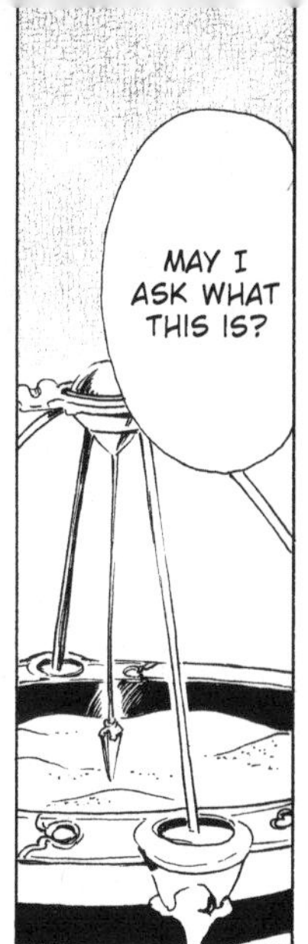
MAY I ASK WHAT THIS IS?

I USE IT IN MY WORK.

YOUR WORK?
AND WHAT SORT OF WORK IS IT THAT YOU DO?

FORTUNE-TELLING.

SO YOU'RE A FORTUNE-TELLER, GRANDMA?!

NOW... KOBATO-CHAN, IT'S YOUR TURN.
AH! RIGHT!

I'M SORRY TO HAVE INTRUDED ON YOU FOR THIS LONG!
BUT EVEN THOUGH YOU SAID YOU NEEDED HELP, WE JUST ENDED UP PLAYING AROUND WITH YOU THE WHOLE TIME...
AND THAT'S EXACTLY WHAT NEW YEAR'S DAY IS ALL ABOUT.

SO THAT THE NEW YEAR MAY TURN OUT FINE AND DANDY AND ONE IS ABLE TO WORK TO THEIR FULLEST ...
...THE LITTLE BREAK FOR RELAXATION AND FUN THAT IS NEW YEAR'S DAY IS ESSENTIAL.
AWWW! THERE WAS SO MUCH SAKE, AND I DIDN'T GET TO DRINK A DROP OF IT! OR EAT ANY OF THAT TASTY-LOOKING MOCHI! AWWWW, MAN...
HERE.
?
お年玉
BAG: OTOSHIDAMA
EH?
EH?
EH?
お年玉
SAKE: HAPPY NEW YEAR
THESE DAYS, IT'S BECOME MORE OF THE CUSTOM TO GIVE MONEY, BUT BACK IN THE OLD DAYS, IT WAS COMMON TO GIVE BALLS OF MOCHI ON NEW YEAR'S.
MOCHI'S BETTER, DON'T YOU THINK?
AND LET'S INCLUDE THIS AS WELL.
THIS IS FOR THAT ADORABLE LITTLE FRIEND OF YOURS WHO HAS A TASTE FOR ALCOHOL.

......YA GOT ME, HUH?
THEY SAY THAT AS YOU GET ON IN YEARS...
...YOU GET TO KNOW JUST A LITTLE MORE ABOUT THE WORLD THAN YOUNG FOLKS DO.
I HOPE YOUR WISH COMES TRUE, KOBATO-CHAN.
...... GRAND-MA...
THANK YOU SO MUCH!!

BUT AS YOU COME ACROSS MORE PEOPLE FROM NOW ON, I THINK YOU MAY FIND YOUR WISH CHANGING A BIT.

Kobato.
Ch. 5
Chocolate and Valentines

WOOOOOOW!!

THE TOWN IS COVERED IN HEARTS AND RIBBONS!
IO-RYOGI-SAN!!
'COS TODAY'S VALENTINE'S DAY.
I KNOW ALL ABOUT VALEN-TINE'S DAY!
IT'S THE DAY YOU GIVE CHOCOLATES TO THE ONE YOU LOVE!
おっ
OH!
THAT'S QUITE AN INFORMED COMMENT FROM YOU, KOBATO!
WELL, I DID MY RESEARCH! WATCHING TV!
BUT WERE VALEN-SAN AND TINE-SAN TWINS?
OR MAYBE THEY WERE JUST BROTHERS?
BUT IT'S A DAY FOR BOTH VALEN-SAN AND TINE-SAN, SO THEY MUST BE GOOD FRIENDS, AT LEAST...
YOU CALL THAT RESEARCH ?!

SIGN: EUROPEAN BAKERY TIROL
欧風菓子 チロル
BOXES: CHAMPAGNE AND SOFT CHOCOLATE SET / CHOCOLATE CIGARETTES
生チョコレート シャンパン
シガレット チョコレート
SORRY TO KEEP YOU WAITING!
I'M SURE EVERYONE AT THE YOMOGI KINDER-GARTEN WILL BE THRILLED TO RECEIVE CHOCOLATES FROM YOU, SAYAKA-SENSEI!

THEY WILL BE THRILLED BECAUSE THEY'RE FOND OF ANYTHING AND EVERY-THING FROM "TIROL."
THANK YOU!
I SHOULD BE THE ONE THANKING YOU FOR THE DISCOUNT.
YOU MIGHT WANT TO THANK FUJIMOTO-KUN FOR THAT.
EH?
WE HAD A LOT OF CHOCOLATES TO PREP FOR VALENTINE'S DAY, AND FUJIMOTO-KUN LENT US A HAND!
THE DISCOUNT IS REALLY A "THANK YOU" TO HIM FOR HELPING US ON TOP OF ALL HIS OTHER JOBS.
IS THAT SO...

OH, AND ...
...THIS.
EH?
I'VE SEEN YOU LOOKING AT THESE, SO I THOUGHT THEY MIGHT BE A FAVO-RITE OF YOURS.
EH! BUT ......
THEY'RE ON THE HOUSE.
BY ALL MEANS, PLEASE COME VISIT US AGAIN.
FUJIMOTO-KUN TOO.
......I WILL.

VALENTINE'S DAY IS...
...THE DAY OF VALENTINE-SAN, SO...
えぐ EGU (STEAM)
えぐ EGU
OKAY, I'VE MEMORIZED IIIIIT!
GEEZ! I ALWAYS END UP THE STRAIGHT MAN IN YOUR COMEDY ROUTINE SINCE THAT HEAD OF YOURS IS FULL OF NOTHING BUT DUMB LINES! FILL YOUR HEAD WITH SOME-THING USEFUL INSTEAD!
...I MUST NOT BREAK UP THE VALENTINE NAME.
I MUST NOT BREAK IT UP.
ほて HOTE
ほて HOTE (PLOD)

DID I REALLY STARE AT IT FOR THAT LONG?
AND HERE I THOUGHT I'D COMPLETELY FORGOTTEN HOW MUCH HE LIKED THESE......
GOSH, I HAVE TO GET BACK TO THE KIDS...

AH!
THERE'S SOMETHING NEAR THE BENCH!
LOOKS LIKE CHOCOLATE.
PISU (SNIFF)
PISU
TODAY IS VALENTINE'S DAY.
SO THAT MUST MEAN SOMEONE PICKED THESE OUT ESPECIALLY FOR SOMEONE ELSE, RIGHT?!

IT'S A REAL POSSI-BILITY.
BUT HERE THEY ARE!
ふあ〜
FUAA (YAWN)
AND NOT A SOUL AROUND!
THIS IS A LOST ITEM, RIGHT?!
AND WHEN YOU FIND A LOST ITEM, WHAT DO YOU DO?!!
CHOCO-LATE!
ISN'T THERE ANYONE AROUND WHO DROPPED THEIR CHOCO-LAAATE!!?
HEY!
HOLD UP!
THERE'S NO ANSWER! PERHAPS THEY'VE MOVED TO SOME FAR-OFF LOCATION!
NO... WHAT I'M SAYING IS...
WHOOOA~?!
WHERE ARE YOU, MISSING-CHOCOLATE PERRRSON?!

I'M BACK.
SIGN: YOMOGI KINDERGARTEN
WEL-COME BACK.
I'M SORRY FOR LEAVING YOU TO HANDLE NAP TIME ALL ON YOUR OWN.
IT'S ALL RIGHT.
THEY WERE ALL VERY GOOD, SO IT WAS NO PROBLEM AT ALL.
HERE, LET ME GET THAT FOR YOU.
THANK YOU.
AND ALSO THANK YOU SO MUCH FOR GOING OVER TO HELP OUT AT "TIROL."
OH... IT WAS NOTHING.

IT'S NOT LIKE THAT.
FUJIMOTO-KUN, IT SEEMS THE MORE EMBARRASSED YOU ARE, THE GRUFFER YOU GET.
AH.
IS SOMETHING WRONG?
NUH-UH, IT'S NOTHING.
WELL, I'M GOING TO PUT ON MY APRON, SO WOULD YOU MIND GOING ON AHEAD?
AH, OKAY.
......COULD I HAVE DROPPED IT?
I FEEL SORRY FOR THE MANAGER AT "TIROL"...... BUT MAYBE IT'S MEANT TO BE THIS WAY.

I COULDN'T FIND THE PERSON ANY-WHERE.....
THE ONE WHO DROPPED THE CHOCOLATE...

WELL, WHATEVER. YOU'RE OUTTA TIME ANYWAY.
AAH! VALENTINE'S DAY IS OVERRR!!
UM, UM! WHAT SHOULD I HAVE DONE WHEN FINDING A LOST ITEM?!

WHEN YOU FIND SUCH AN ITEM, TRYING TO FIND ITS OWNER IS THE CORRECT COURSE OF ACTION.
SO THEN MY SCORE WILL BE ...?!

HOWEVER! WOULD IT NOT HAVE BEEN MUCH QUICKER IF YOU'D SIMPLY TURNED IT IN TO THE POLICE RATHER THAN RUNNING ALL OVER TOWN? HUUUH?!
EHH?!

COME HERE, KOBATO.
THIRTY-FIVE POINTS!
35
N-NEXT TIME, FOR SURE—!!
35
ボリ ボリ
BORI (CRUNCH)
BORI
OKAY, VALENTINE'S DAY'S OVER NOW, SO...
...WE CAN EAT THE CHOCO-LATES, RIGHT?

Kobato.
Ch. 6
What Does Ohanami mean?

THE SAKURA TREES ARE IN FULL BLOOM!
IORYOGI-SAN!
YEAH... SURE LOOKS LIKE IT.
AND WHAT DOES "SAKURA IN FULL BLOOM" MEAN?!
HANAMI!

AND WHAT'S "HANAMI" MEAN?!
FLOWER VIEWING PARTIES!!
YOU GOT IT!
CONTRARY TO EXPECTATION, YOU DO KNOW A THING OR TWO, DON'TCHA, KOBATO?
BECAUSE I DID MY RESEARCH!
BY WATCHING TV AND READING MAGAZINES AND STUFF!
ALL RIGHT!
IN THAT CASE, YOU SHOULD ALREADY BE FAMILIAR WITH THE MOST APPROPRIATE ACTIONS TO TAKE DURING FLOWER VIEWING, YES?!

BUT OF COURSE!!
すとん
SUTON (FWUMP)
WHAT ARE YOU DOING?
UM...I'M SAVING A SPOT—
ビクッ
BIKU (FLINCH)
......
WHAT ARE YOU FLINCHING FOR?

NO, U-UM...
I THOUGHT YOU MIGHT GO "GRRAAAAH" WITH THE FIRE LIKE YOU ALWAYS DO, IORYOGI-SAN...
BIKU
BIKU
I'M NOT GONNA ROAST YOU. AFTER ALL, SAVING A SPOT IS WHAT PEOPLE USUALLY DO, RIGHT?
YOU DEFINITELY NEED A GOOD FLOWER-VIEWING SPOT FOR HANAMI.
YUP, YUP.
THEN WHAT I DID WAS RIGHT...AND I PASS?!
NOPE, SAVING A SPOT IS JUST THE BEGINNING!
THERE ARE STILL MORE APPROPRIATE BEHAVIORS FOR HANAMI!
APPROPRIATE BEHAVIORS FOR HANAMI ......?
NOW! SHOW ME YOUR HANAMI COMMON SENSE!!
KOBA—!
OH!
SIS, YOU SURE ARE CUUUUTE!
COME OVER HERE AND DRINK WITH US!
ZUI
ZUI (ZIP)
ZUI
WHOA!!
EH?
EH?!

AND ON THAT NOTE...

YOU'RE RIGHT. IT WOULD BE A REAL PROBLEM IF THE KINDERGARTNERS WERE GIVEN A HARD TIME BY A BUNCH OF DRUNKARDS!
LET'S TRY OVER THERE.
OKAY.
GO ON, DRINK IT DOWN!
NOW EAT THIS ALL UP!
NO, REALLY, I...
NO, I'M STILL TOO—
GASHI (GRAB)

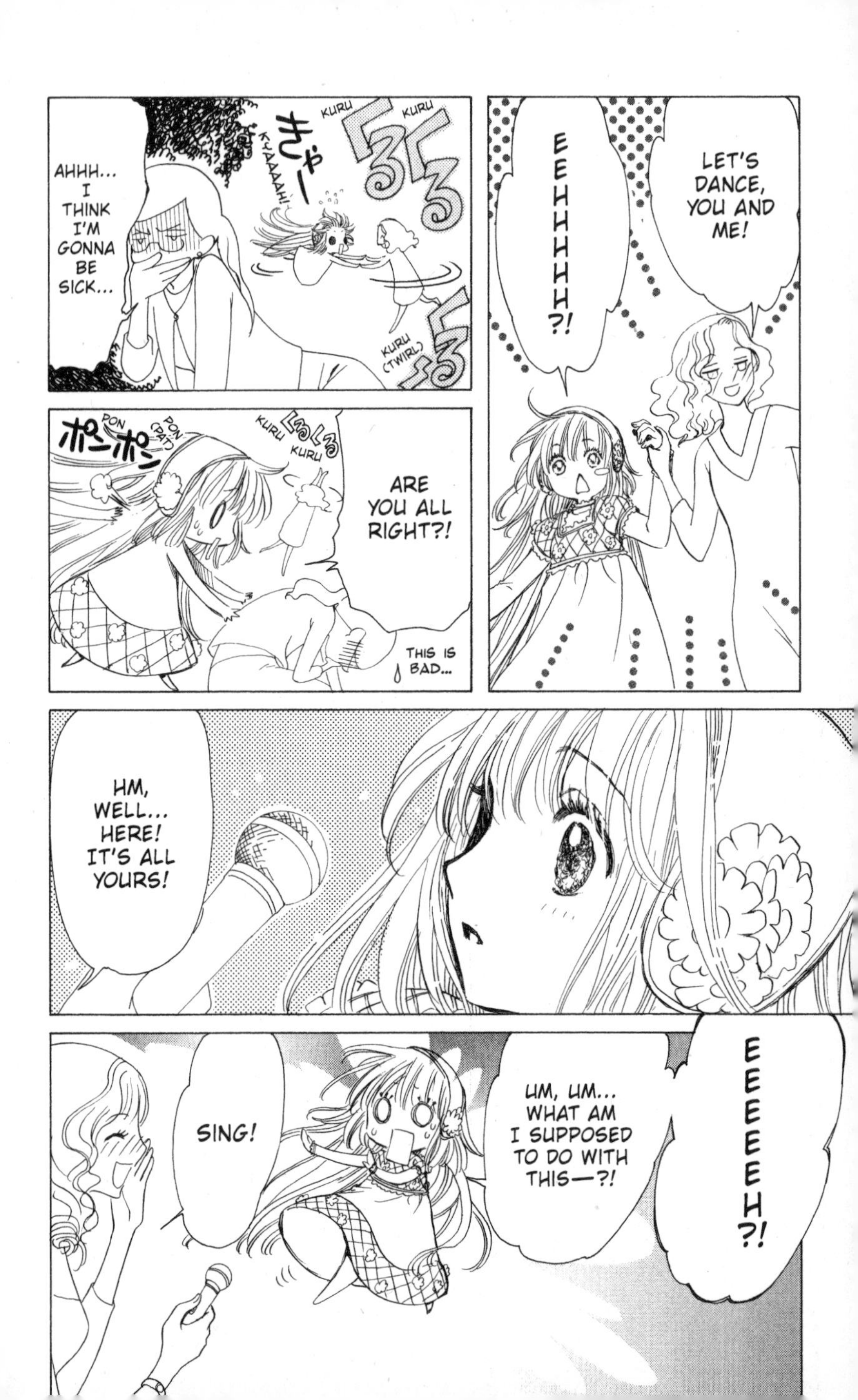
LET'S DANCE, YOU AND ME!
EEHHHHHH?!
KURU KURU
KYAAAAAH!
KURU (TWIRL)
AHHH... I THINK I'M GONNA BE SICK...
KURU KURU
PON PON (PAT)
ARE YOU ALL RIGHT?!
THIS IS BAD...
HM, WELL... HERE! IT'S ALL YOURS!
EEEEEEH?!
UM, UM... WHAT AM I SUPPOSED TO DO WITH THIS—?!
SING!

M-MIGHT SINGING BE A CUSTOM AT HANAMI PARTIES?!
OF COURSE!
YO! WE'RE WAITING ON YOU!!
BUT, BUT... I'M NOT SURE MY SINGING WILL BE APPROPRIATE FOR AN OCCASION LIKE THIS!
WE'RE NOT PICKY!
JUST SING ANY-THING!
WHAT OUR BOSS JUST DID TO HIS SONG IS FAR WORSE THAN ANY-THING YOU COULD DO!
I-IS THAT RIGHT?
はははは
HA HA HA HA!
O—
OKAY THEN...!!

GUI
(YANK)
...IS THAT KOBATO?
WELL... AT LEAST SHE CAN CARRY A TUNE.

U-UMM ...
DID I DO SOMETHING ODD?
わあっ
WOW!
THAT WAS GREAT!
SING ANOTHER ONE!
SO GOOD!
O-OKAAAY?!
I WONDER WHO'S SINGING?
BEATS ME.
STILL, IT'S JUST WONDERFUL!

SINGING AT A HANAMI PARTY, HM?
WELL, IT CERTAINLY IS APPROPRIATE FOR THE OCCASION.
ADD IN THE SAKURA TREES BEING IN FULL BLOOM, AND...
KOBATO, THIS TIME, YOU GET NINETY-FIVE POINTS!

Kobato.
Ch. 7
Kobato on a Rainy Day

IT'S RAINING, HUH?
IT'S RAINING, YEAH.
AND YOU KNOW ALL ABOUT THE RIGHT THINGS TO DO...
...ON A RAINY DAY, DON'T YOU KOBATO?
OF COURSE I DO, IORYOGI-SAN!
GABA (BOLT)

KYAN!
GO (WHACK)
YORO (STAGGER)
YORO
GASA (RUSTLE)
MAYBE THERE'S ONE HERE ...?
OR MAYBE OVER HERE ...?
GASA
...AND EXACTLY WHAT MIGHT YOU BE SEARCHING FOR, KOBATO-KUN?
A LEAF!
KIND OF LIKE THIS!
YA THINK YER ONE OF THOSE LEGENDARY AINU DWARVES OR SOME-THING?!!
GOOOOOO (BLAAAAST)

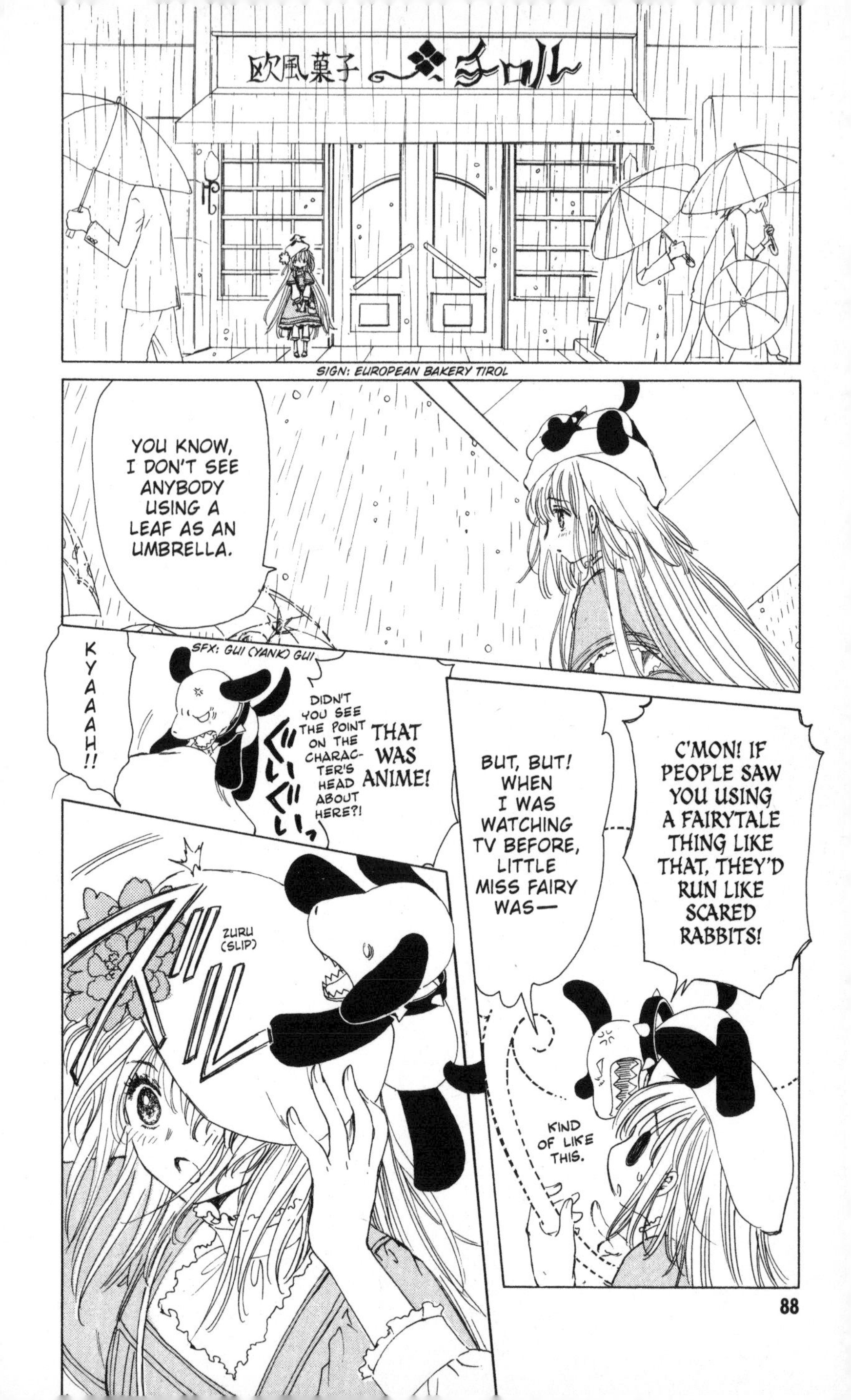
欧風菓子 チロル
SIGN: EUROPEAN BAKERY TIROL
YOU KNOW, I DON'T SEE ANYBODY USING A LEAF AS AN UMBRELLA.
C'MON! IF PEOPLE SAW YOU USING A FAIRYTALE THING LIKE THAT, THEY'D RUN LIKE SCARED RABBITS!
BUT, BUT! WHEN I WAS WATCHING TV BEFORE, LITTLE MISS FAIRY WAS—
KIND OF LIKE THIS.
THAT WAS ANIME!
DIDN'T YOU SEE THE POINT ON THE CHARACTER'S HEAD ABOUT HERE?!
SFX: GUI (YANK) GUI
KYAAAAH!!
ZURU (SLIP)

KYAH!
THAT WAS CLOSE, HUH?
Y—
YES, IT WAS...
DON'T YOU EVER...
...TAKE OFF YOUR HAT! GOT IT?
YES, SIR.

HI THERE.
GOOD DAY.
PEKO (BOW)
WHY, YOU'RE THE YOUNG LADY WHO HELPED US OUT AT CHRIST-MASTIME!
YOU REMEM-BERED ME!
OF COURSE!
TAKING SHELTER FROM THE RAIN?
Y— YES.
CALLING IT "TAKING SHELTER" IS OKAY, RIGHT?
RIGHT.
HERE!

PLEASE USE THIS IF YOU'D LIKE.
BUT, BUT...
I HAVEN'T GOT ANY MONEY, SO...
IT'S MY PRESENT TO YOU.
BUT SINCE IT'S JUST A PLASTIC UMBRELLA, IT ISN'T MUCH OF A PRESENT.
......
UM, UM!
WOULD IT BE OKAY IF I JUST BORROWED IT?
I WILL COME AND RETURN IT WHEN THE RAIN LETS UP!
VERY WELL. I'LL WAIT FOR YOUR RETURN.
THANK YOU SO MUCH!

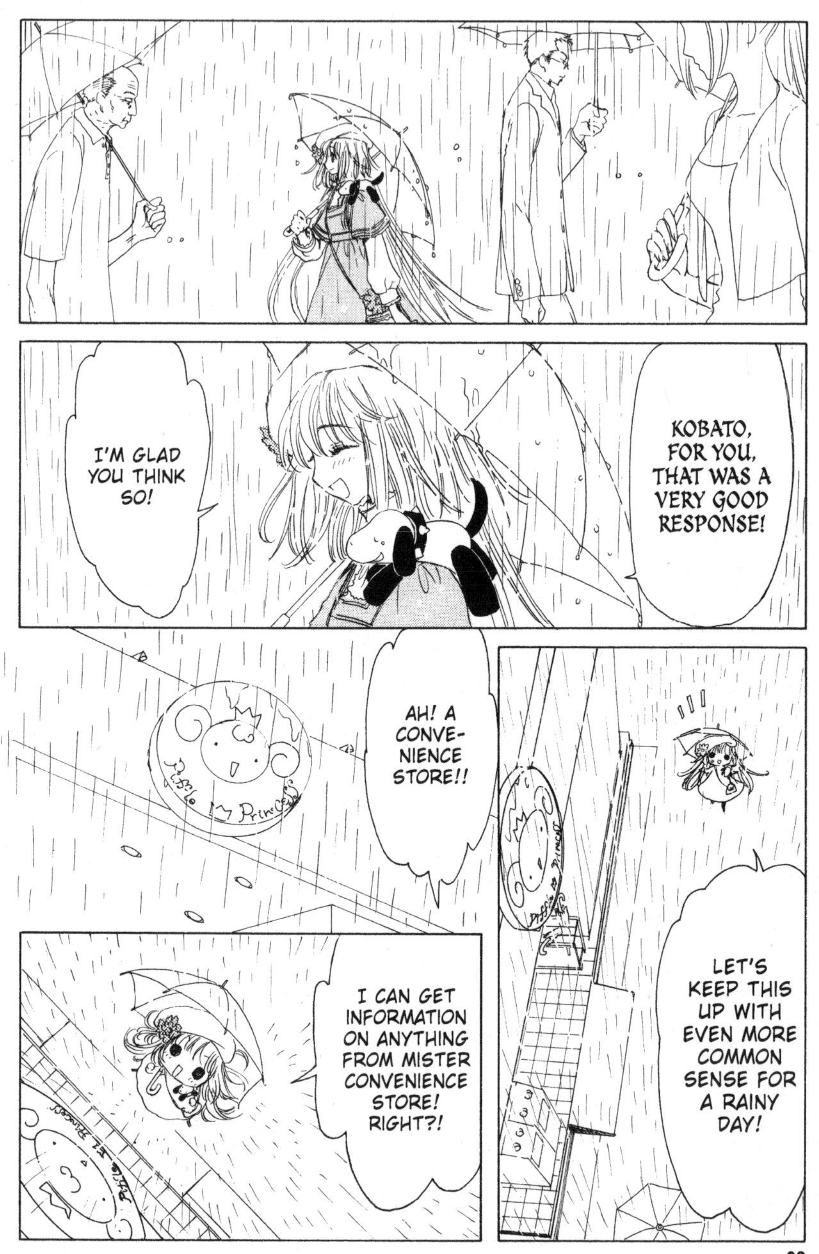
KOBATO, FOR YOU, THAT WAS A VERY GOOD RESPONSE!
I'M GLAD YOU THINK SO!
LET'S KEEP THIS UP WITH EVEN MORE COMMON SENSE FOR A RAINY DAY!
AH! A CONVE-NIENCE STORE!!
I CAN GET INFORMATION ON ANYTHING FROM MISTER CONVENIENCE STORE! RIGHT?!

THAT'S SORT OF TRUE... MAYBE?
AFTER ALL, IT IS THIS TOWN'S "HOT STATION!"
I'LL COLLECT A WHOLE BUNCH OF SCOOPS ABOUT RAINY DAY ETIQUETTE RIGHT AWAY!
KOBATO IS ON THE CASE!
KATAN (CLACK)

THAT WAS TERRIFIC! I PICKED UP ALL KINDS OF NEW THINGS ABOUT RAINY DAYS!
OH YEAH?
BUT THIS CONVE-NIENCE STORE DOESN'T CARRY BOOZE!
AH?
WHAT IS IT, IORYOGI-SAN?
THE UMBRELLA. IT'S GONE.
EH ?!

YOU'RE RIGHT! THE UMBRELLA ISN'T HERE ANYMORE!!
YEAH...
PERHAPS SOMEONE TOOK IT BY MISTAKE?!
NAH. THE RAIN WAS PRETTY SUDDEN, SO SOMEBODY WITHOUT ONE PROB-ABLY JUST WALKED OFF WITH IT.
EH ?!
DOES THAT MEAN THAT ALL UMBRELLAS ARE THERE FOR THE TAKING?
NO WAY!
THEN WHY ...?
HMMM... WELL, I'D EXPECT IT'S 'COS WHOEVER TOOK IT DIDN'T WANNA GET WET.
BUT THAT MAKES TROUBLE FOR THE UMBRELLA'S RIGHTFUL OWNER!
WELL, THERE ARE STILL PEOPLE OUT THERE WHO ONLY THINK ABOUT THEM-SELVES.

WHAT'S WRONG?
UM, UM...
M—
MY UMBRELLA...
IT ISN'T THERE ANYMORE?
...BUT THAT'S...
AND AFTER THE BAKERY'S PROPRIETOR WAS SO KIND AS TO LEND IT TO ME...
SU (PUSH)
I'LL GIVE YOU THIS ONE!
B—
BUT!
...YES.

HERE!
TH—
THANK YOU VERY MUCH!
DON'T WORRY!
HE AND I CAN SHARE!

GIVE SOMETHING TO SOMEBODY YOU KNOW. GIVE SOMETHING TO SOMEBODY YOU DON'T KNOW.

TAKE SOMETHING FROM SOMEBODY YOU DON'T KNOW. TAKE SOMETHING FROM SOMEBODY YOU KNOW.

THIS GOES TO SHOW THAT THE WOUNDS OF EACH HEART YOU NEED TO HELP WILL BE DIFFERENT FROM THE NEXT.
UNTIL YOU CAN UNDERSTAND THAT, YOU CAN'T HELP ANY OF THEM.
...YES.
WELL, WHETHER YOU GET THAT OR NOT, YOU STILL HAVE TO GET YOUR HANDS ON THAT BOTTLE FIRST.
YES! AND HOW DID I DO TODAY?!
LESSEE... YOU DID UNEXPECTEDLY WELL THIS TIME, SO—
WAH!
ARE YOU ALL RIGHT, IORYOGI-SAN?!
KYAAAAH!!
FOREHEAD: 0 POINTS
0点
EEEEH?!
BA (WHAP) BA
THAT'S AN AWFUL THING TO DO! IORYOGI-SAAAN!

Kobato.
Ch. 8
Ioryogi-san and Mister Beer

MIIIN (BZZZ)
MIIIN
JIRI
JIRI
JIRI (ZZZ)
... I!!!!!! OOO...
... RYOOO ...
... GI!!!! ...
... SAAAN ...
MIIIN
MIIIN
IIIIT'S ... ... SOOOO HOOOT ...
MIIIN
STOP SHOVING THINGS INTO MY FACE THAT I CAN'T DO A THING ABOUT!
MIIIN

BUUUT... IT'S HOT, SO...
...AT LEAST SAYING IIIT...
...MAKES ME FEEL A LITTLE BETTER-RRR...
...AND MAKES ME FEEL COOLER-RRRR!
GOOOO (ROOOAR)
ARRRGH! YOU'RE GETTING ON MY NERVES!!
あつ HOT!
あつ HOT!
あつ HOT!
あづ〜〜 HOTTT!
ENOUGH! YOU'RE JUST MAKING IT FEEL HOTTER!
I'M SORRY-YYYY!

I KNOW! LET'S GO DRINK SOME WATER.
KA (SHINE)
YORO (WOBBLE) YORO
SFX: JIRI (BUZZ) JIRI JIRI JIRI
LISTEN UP, YOU FOOL!
ISN'T IT OBVIOUS THAT IF YOU GO TO A PLACE THAT'S BAKED BY THE SUN, THE WATER WILL PROBABLY BE JUST AS HOT AND WON'T DO YOU A BIT OF GOOD?!
IS THAT RIGHT?
ON THE OTHER HAND, IF WE DON'T STAY HYDRATED, IT COULD PUT OUR LIVES IN DANGER.
BUT IF WE CAN'T DRINK THE WATER FROM THE PARK FOUNTAIN, THEN WHAT SHOULD WE DRINK ...?
BEER!!
KIRAN (GLINT)

...AND...
THIS IS THE KIND OF DAY WHERE WE QUICKLY MAKE OUR WAY TO A NICE, FROSTY BEER...
...GULP IT DOWN ...!!!!
...LIKE THIS!!!
GO GO GO (GLUG)
PUHAAH!
I WANT ONE RIGHT NOW !!!
PACHI
PACHI
PACHI (CLAP)

SEE, THAT RIGHT THERE'S THE PROB-LEM!!
HERO (SLUMP)
HERO
BUT, BUT WE CAN'T BUY MISTER BEER WITHOUT MONEYYY!
PACHI (CLAP)
PACHI
WHEN TRYING TO COUNTER GLOBAL WARMING, RATHER THAN SOME LAME "COOL BIZ" CAMPAIGN...
...IT WOULD BE FAR MORE EFFECTIVE TO DOLE OUT FREE BEER AT ALL THE NATION'S BEER GARDENS!!
AS LONG AS A PERSON'S GOT A FROSTY MUG OF BEER, THEY CAN HANDLE AN EXTRA FIVE DEGREES OVER THE DICTATED A/C TEMPERATURE LIMITS!
NO! THEY'D PREFER IT THAT WAY!
F-FOR SOME REASON, YOU SEEM A LITTLE DIFFERENT TODAY THAN MOST DAYS —!

KURA (DIZZY)
KURA
THAT TELLS YOU HOW BAD I WANT A BEER!!
I'VE GOT IT!
EVERY NOW AND AGAIN, MISTER SHOPPING DISTRICT GIVES AWAY STUFF! FOR FREE!
YEAH... THOSE ARE JUST FREE SAMPLES.
PIKU (PERK)
BUT WOULDN'T THEY GIVE AWAY SAMPLES OF MISTER BEER TOO ?!
YESSS.
THAT HAS BEEN KNOWN TO HAPPEN.
THEN HOW ABOUT WE GET A SAMPLE OF MISTER BEER?!

YEAAAH... I GOT NO GRIPES ABOUT THAT BIT OF SUMMERTIME COMMON SENSE.
BETTER YET, IT'S THE RIGHT THING TO DO!
YOU COULD EVEN CALL IT AN "HEROIC" ACTION.
JIRI (BUZZ)
JIRI
THEN I'M OFF TO GET A FREE MISTER BEER!!
HEY—
OH!
WAI—
GABA (LURCH)
TA (TAP) TA TA
たったったっ
I'M SURPRISED SHE CAN RUN IN THIS HEAT.
MIIIN MIIIN (BUZZ)
HOW PATHETIC YOU LOOK!

......I DON'T WANNA HEAR IT FROM YOU, YA BASTARD.
GINSEI.
WHAT'S WITH THIS "IORYOGI-SAN" CRAP? IT'S NOT JUST THE WAY YOU LOOK THAT'S PATHETIC, IT'S YOUR NEW NAME TOO.
I HAVE TO SAY THAT I LIKE THIS FORM. AND THE NAME THAT GOES WITH IT.

SO YOU'RE SAYING YOU THREW AWAY YOUR NAME?
THINK WHAT YOU LIKE.
....
......LAY A FINGER ON KOBATO, AND I'LL WRING YOUR NECK, WE CLEAR?!
DO YOU THINK YOU CAN? THE WAY YOU ARE NOW?
WANNA TRY ME?

ZA (SWSH)
ZA
BA (LEAP)
ZA (SKID)
SHA (SWOOSH)

GA
(WHACK)
TO
(TMP)
PAN
(SMACK)
DOSA
(THUD)
DON
(BAM)

LOOKS LIKE I CAN STILL WRING YER NECK, EVEN AS I AM NOW.
MAYBE I OUGHTA JUST FRY YA RIGHT HERE, HUH?!
GABA (LURCH)
WHOA!
THOUGH YOUR TECH-NIQUES ARE AS GOOD AS EVER, THERE'S NO WAY YOU COULD EVER KEEP ME DOWN IN THAT FORM.
WHOOOA! I FORGOT ABOUT THAT!

SA (WSH)
DON'T YOU FORGET. I'M GOING TO FINISH MY BUSINESS WITH YOU SOMEDAY, NO MATTER WHAT!
GASA (RUSTLE)
ZA (SWOOSH)
SAAA (WSHHH)
...... WHAT A PAIN.

Kobato.
Ch. 9
The Test Results Are In?!

MISTER BEER!
MISTER BEER, WHERE ARE YOU?
ISN'T THERE ANY MISTER BEER AROUND?
COME ONE, COME ALL!
YOU WON'T TASTE ANYTHING BETTER!

PLEASE HAVE SOOOME!
IT'S SO NICE AND COLDDD!
DA (DASH)
ONE COLD, FROSTY B—
HERE!
HAVE A TASTE OF OUR LATEST ICE CREAM!
NOT... MISTER BEER.

WOULD YOU LIKE TO TRY THIS?
OUR LATEST ICE CREAM!
しょぼん…
SHOBON (SAD)

WE'VE GOT DELICIOUS, ICE-COLD BEER OVER HERE!!
PIKU (PERK)

HERE YOU GO!
WE'RE UNDERAGE! SHOULD WE REALLY BE HANDIN' OUT BEER?
WELL, IT'S NOT LIKE WE'RE DRINKING IT, RIGHT?
SFX: DOKI (BADUM) DOKI

GARA (CLUNK)
GARA
WE'RE DOWN TO THE LAST FEW. I'LL GO GET MORE.
OKAAAAY! THANKS!
TA (TMP)
TA
TA
YES, PLEASE!!
OKAAAAAY!!

IT'S ICE-COLD MISTER BEEEEER!
ペコリ
PEKORI (BOW)
THANK YOU SO VERY, VERY MUCH!!
WITH THIS, IORYOGI-SAN'S GLOBAL WARMING WILL BE SOLVED TOO!!
タタタ
TA (TMP) TA TA

MAAAN, HAVING A PERSON BE THAT HAPPY MAKES HANDING OUT THIS STUFF WORTH IT!
Y- Y- Y— YEAH!

DID SOMETHING HAPPEN?
BEER
生

IT SEEMS OUR BEER WILL HELP WITH GLOBAL WARMING, IORYOGI-SAN'S GLOBAL WARMING.

IORYOGI?
?
BEER
生

IORYOGI-SAAAN!
KYAAAAAAH!!
PLEASE HANG IN THERE! IORYOGI-SAN!
I'VE BROUGHT YOU SOME BEER!!!
KASA KASA (RUSTLE)
WELL DONE, KOBATO-OOO!!!
BEER

GO ON, PLEASE HAVE SOME!!
KASHI (PSHHT)
PUSHUU (BLAST)
IDI—!!
KYAAAAAAH!!!!!

SEKIKA (PETRIFIED)
石化!
GOSO (RUMMAGE)
ごそごそ
GOSO
CHA (SWSH)
ちゃっ
KYAAAAAAH!!!!!!
-100
サラリ
SARARI (STROKE)

SFX: HOTO (PLIP) HOTO
ほとほと
ALL MY HARD-EARNED POINTS HAVE BEEN WIPED OUT JUST LIKE THAT!
-100
...OR AT LEAST, THAT'S THE SCORE I'D LIKE TO GIVE YOU, BUT...
...FACTORING IN THE GOOD INTENTIONS THAT SENT YOU RUNNING ALL OVER TOWN JUST TO GET ME A BEER...

THANK YOU SO MUCH!!
AND THAT MEANS...
...KOBATO HANATO...
Y—
YES, SIR?
WHAT IS YOUR WISH?

THERE IS A PLACE I WANT TO GO.

AND TO THAT END, WHAT DO YOU NEED?

I MUST FILL UP A "BOTTLE" TO THE BRIM WITH WOUNDED HEARTS.

AND BEFORE YOU CAN DO THAT ...?
I MUST DO MY BEST TO EARN THAT "BOTTLE" ...

TH...IS...
KOBATO, YOU PASS.
EH...?!
IF YOU DON'T WANT IT, GIVE IT BACK!
NOOOOO, I NEED IT!!
SO IF I FILL THIS "BOTTLE" UP...
...I CAN GO...

BUT LISTEN UP. YOU'VE ONLY JUST PASSED THE FIRST ONE, THE "COMMON SENSE" TEST.
I KNOW!
AND TO HEAL WOUNDED HEARTS, IT WON'T DO TO BE HOMELESS, SO...
...WE'LL NEED TO GET OURSELVES A HOME BASE TO START OFF.
'COS IF WE SEEM TOO SUSPICIOUS, THE TARGETS WON'T EVEN TALK TO US.
BESIDES, I'M SICK OF SLEEPING ROUGH.
YES, SIR!
NOW THAT YOU HAVE THE "BOTTLE," THE REAL TRIAL BEGINS!
YES!
YER GONNA HAVE TO PUT YOUR HEART INTO THIS, KOBATO!
KOBATO WILL GIVE IT EVERYTHING SHE'S GOT!!

KOBATO.

THIS IS WHERE IT BEGINS!
MY NEW LIFE!
ふるる
FURU (FWIP)
KOBATO IS GOING TO...
...GIVE IT EVERYTHING SHE'S GOT!

Kobato.
Ch. 10
Please Let Me Heal You!

GON (WHAM)
KYAN!!
UWAH ...
HEY! THERE SHOULD BE LIMITS TO THE USE OF EVEN CLASSIC GAGS!

IORYOGI-SAAAN!
I THINK I CRUSHED MY NOSE.

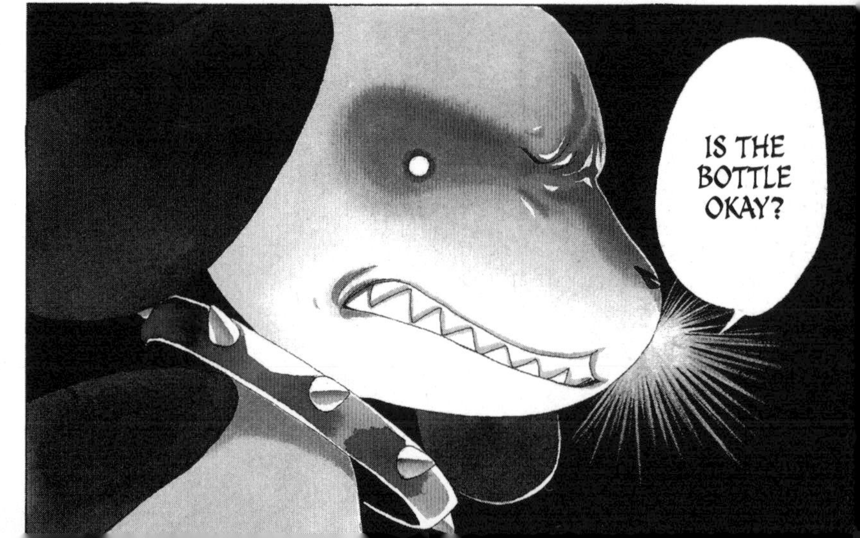
IS THE BOTTLE OKAY?

がばっ
GABA (LURCH)
はっ
HA (GASP)
I- IT'S ALL RIGHT!
GOOD.
IF THAT BOTTLE BREAKS, THEN IT'LL ALL HAVE BEEN FOR NOTHING.
I KNOW!
DON (BAM)
WHAT IS OUR REASON FOR COMING HERE?!

TO FILL THIS BOTTLE TO THE BRIM WITH WOUNDED HEARTS!
AND TO DO THAT?!
I MUST CURE THE HEARTS OF THOSE WHO HAVE BEEN WOUNDED!

HOW?!
I'LL GIVE IT ALL I'VE GOT! YEAHHH!
I'LL! I'LL DO ALL KINDS OF STUFF!!

WHAT KIND OF ANSWER IS THAAAT?!!
AND WHO MIGHT YOU BE?
PITA (FREEZE)
KOOOOO (ROOOAR)
KYAAAAH!!
BURU (TREMBLE) BURU

UH, UM...
SFX: KOSO (WHISPER)
I-I'LL BE LIVING HERE FROM TODAY ON! I'M KOBATO HANATO!
PEKO (BOW)
I'VE BEEN WAITING FOR YOU! SO YOU'RE KOBATO-SAN?
"I'LL BE LIVING HERE FROM TODAY ON. PLEASED TO MAKE YOUR ACQUAIN-TANCE," RIGHT? COME ON!
MY NAME IS CHITOSE MIHARA.
I'M THE MANAGER FOR THIS APART-MENT.
IT IS VERY NICE TO MEET YOU!
SHE SEEMS SOOO NICE!
HOW WONDER-FUL!
YES! VERY NICE TO MEET YOU TOO!!

SFX: GO (RUMBLE) GO GO GO

SO THIS IS MY ROOM.
I HAVE TO DO MY BEST EVERY DAY TO FILL UP THIS BOTTLE JUST AS FAST AS I CAN.
GO GO GO (RUMBLE)
KYAAAH!
DOOO-BAAA-TOOO!
GARA (RATTLE)
GO GO GO GO
YOU MORON! HOW DARE YOU LEAVE ME LIKE THAT?!!

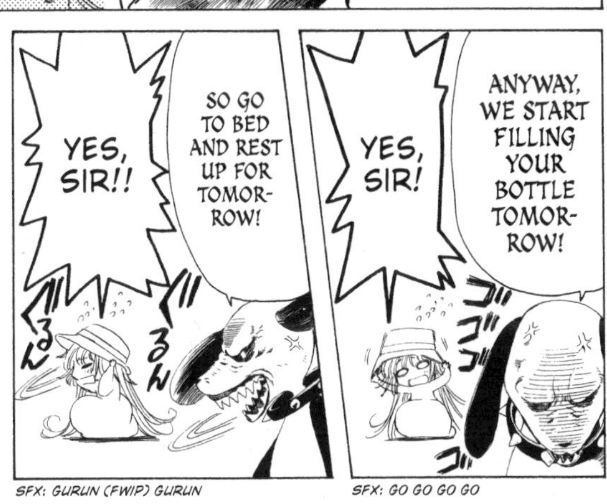

SFX: GURUN (FWIP) GURUN

SFX: GO GO GO GO

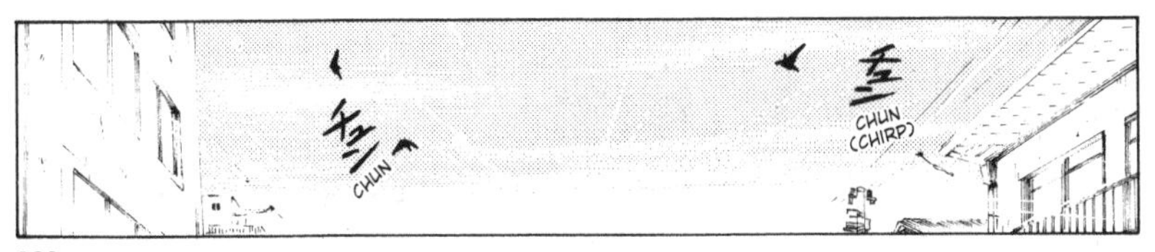

IORYOGI-SAN! IORYOGI-SAN!
ACT NORMAL AND STOP TALKING TO YOUR STUFFED TOY.
I WONDER WHO I SHOULD HEAL FIRST?
きょろ
KYORO (GLANCE)
あ
AH!
UM! ARE YOU WOUNDED ?!
HUH?
IS THERE ANY WAY I MIGHT BE OF HELP?
WH-WHAT ARE YOU TALKING ABOUT ?!

ぱたぱた
PATA
PATA (PATTER)
AH! WAIT, PLEASE!
I WANT TO HEAL YOU!!

ぽつん
POTSUN (ALONE)
...THIS IS A NIGHT-MARE......

AH! OVER THERE! SHE LOOKS LIKE SHE'S IN TROUBLE!!
WAIT A SECOND, HEY!

FUU (SIGH)
NOBODY WANTS ME TO HEAL THEIR HEARTS...
OR RATHER THEY'RE RUNNING FOR THE HILLS WHEN YOU SHOW UP!
DIDN'T I TELL YOU TO WAIT?
PON (PAT)
ARE YOU LOOKING FOR A CLIENT?
EX-CUSE ME?
YOU PROPOSITIONED PEOPLE BACK THERE, RIGHT? HOW MUCH?
NO... I'M NOT TRYING TO DO IT FOR MONEY. I JUST WANTED TO HEAL PEOPLE'S WOUNDED HEARTS, SO...

WHAT? YOU MEAN IT'S FREE?
GO GO GO GO (RUMBLE)
DOES THAT MEAN YOU'LL LET ME HEAL YOU?!
OH YES, I SURE WANT TO BE HEALED!
IN ALL SORTS OF WAYS!
THEN PLEASE LET ME HEAL YOU!!
UIN UIN (WOO) UI UI UI UI
GUI (GRAB)
GREAT! LET'S HURRY OVER THERE!
KUA (ROAR)

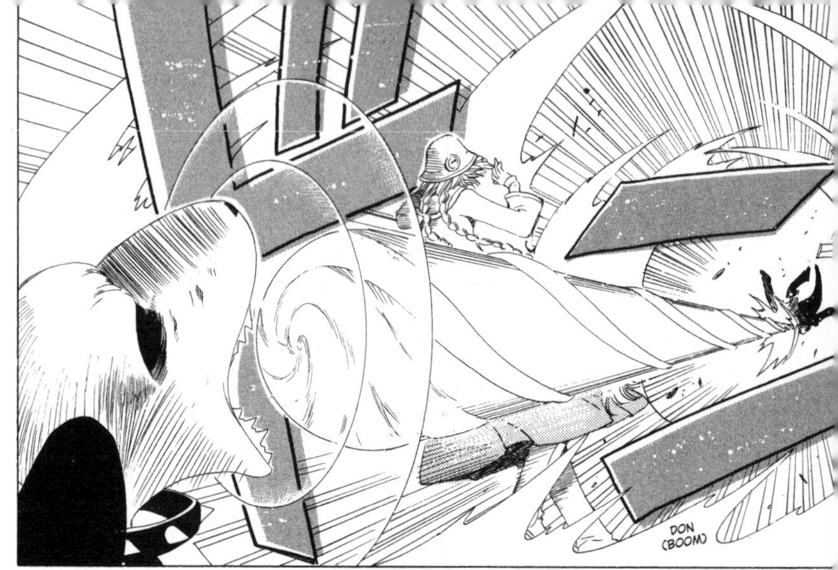

SFX: BIRI (CRACKLE) BIRI

SFX: GUWA (ROAR)

ARE YOU IN CAHOOTS WITH SOME-ONE?!
IS THIS AN EXTOR-TION RACKET ?!
I DON'T UNDER-STAND WHAT YOU'RE TALKING ABOUT!
BA (WHAP)
YOU LITTLE—!!
KYAAAAAH!!
GA (WHACK)

ZUZAA (SLIDE)
IORYOGI-SAN?!

SHUT UP, CREEP!

...TH—
THANK......
LOOK, I DON'T KNOW IF YOU'RE INVOLVED IN ENKOU OR URI...
...JUST DON'T DO IT AROUND HERE!

ぱちくり
PACHIKURI (BLINK)
...HUH?

KOBATO, WE HAVE TO GET OUTTA HERE!
...IORYOGI-SAN...

LIKE I SAID! RUN FOR IT!
URR... RGH...

WHAT ARE "ENKOU" AND "URI"?
ぐはっ
GUHAH!

EEEE-EEH?!
"ENKOU" IS DATES FOR MONEY?!
AND "URI" IS PROSTI-TUTION?! THAT'S WHAT THEY REALLY MEAN?!
WHEN IT COMES TO "CLUELESS," YOU REALLY TAKE THE CAKE, HUH ?!

BUT I SHOULD HAVE EXPECTED NOTHING LESS FROM DOBATO.
IT'S KOBATO!!

TO THINK, I ACTUALLY APPEARED TO BE DOING SOMETHING LIKE THAT —!

FORGET THAT, AND LOOK HERE!
IN AN ENTIRE DAY, YOU'VE MANAGED TO ADD ZILCH TO YOUR BOTTLE.
T-TOMORROW, I'LL REALLY TRY MY BEST!
う…
UUU...

I DIDN'T FIND A SINGLE PERSON WHO WANTED TO BE HEALED!
とぼ
TOBO (TRUDGE)
とぼ
TOBO
THERE ARE SO MANY SEEMINGLY WOUNDED PEOPLE OUT THERE, BUT NONE OF THEM WOULD LET ME DO ANYTHING......

IT'S THAT PERSISTENT APPROACH OF YOURS, RUSHING RIGHT UP TO THEM AND SHOUTING, "PLEASE LET ME HEAL YOU!"
BUT IF I DON'T GATHER UP WOUNDED HEARTS......
...THE BOTTLE WILL......
!!
ばさっ
BASA (FWAP)
KYAAAAAH!!
すってん
SUTTON (THUNK)
THE SHEET WENT FLYING—!!
BUT TO WHERE—?!
ぱた
PATA
ぱた
PATA (PATTER)
SIS! WHATCHA DOING?
わたわた
WATA WATA (FLAIL)

ARE YOU OKAY?
Y-YES ...

AH HA HA!
あはは
WAAAH! SHE'S GOT A RED MARK ON HER NOSE!
YOU'RE RIIIGHT!
NOW, NOW! IT'S NOT NICE TO LAUGH AT PEOPLE!
'KAAAY, SAYAKA-SENNN-SEEEH!
PLEASE FORGIVE US.
I WORK OVER THERE AT THE YOMOGI KINDER-GARTEN.
WE'RE A LITTLE SHORTHANDED, AND I WAS LATE GETTING ALL THE LAUNDRY OFF THE LINE BEFORE...
YOU DON'T HAVE ENOUGH HELP?!
TH-THAT'S RIGHT.
THEN YOU HAVE TROU-BLES?
Y-YOU COULD SAY THAT.

SO IF YOU HAD HELP, THAT WOULD BE A CURE?!
KIRA
KIRA (SPARKLE)
WELL ......
WOULD IT BE A CURE?!
BA (LUNGE)
A-AH... YES, I SUPPOSE IT WOULD.
THEN PLEASE ALLOW ME TO HELP!
SIGN: YOMOGI KINDERGARTEN
YOU SEE HOW OLD THIS PLACE IS?
KOTO (CLINK)
THERE'S A BRAND-NEW KINDERGARTEN NEARBY, SO...
...WE DON'T HAVE AS MANY CHILDREN AS BE-FORE.

I HAVEN'T BEEN ABLE TO HIRE ANY NEW LICENSED PROVIDERS, SO...
YOU MEAN, IF I'M NOT A LICENSED PROVIDER, I CAN'T HELP?!
THAT ISN'T IT. WHAT I NEED MOST RIGHT NOW IS SOMEBODY TO HELP WITH STUFF LIKE THE CLEANING AND LAUNDRY.
BUT THE PAY WILL BE...
I DON'T MIND ABOUT THAT!
AS LONG AS I CAN CURE A WOUNDED HEART!
KUSU (CHUCKLE)
くす
KUSU
くす
YOU'RE A VERY INTER-ESTING GIRL.
WHAT'S YOUR NAME?
KOBATO HANATO!

I'M SAYAKA OKIURA.
WELL THEN, CAN I ASK YOU TO BE MY NEW ASSISTANT?
YES!!
YOU SHOULDN'T BE HIRING SOME WEIRDO OFF THE STREET SO CARE-LESSLY...
...SAYAKA-SENSEI.
はっ
HA (GASP)

IT'S YOU!
THE DATES FOR MONEY PROSTITUTE GUY!!

WHAT'S THAT SUPPOSED TO MEAN?
BISHI (WHIP)

ARE YOU TWO FRIENDS?

NO, WE ARE NOT!

THIS IS KIYOKAZU FUJIMOTO-KUN. YOU AND HE WILL BE WORKING TOGETHER.

THE REALITY IS THAT WE'RE SHORT-HANDED.
AND SHE DOESN'T SEEM LIKE A BAD PERSON.
KOKU (NOD)
KOKU
KOKU
BAD PEOPLE DON'T GO AROUND LOOKING LIKE BAD PEOPLE, RIGHT?
HMPH!
MU (IRK)
BUT I'VE ALREADY ASKED HER, AND SHE ACCEPTED, SO...
WE'LL EXPECT YOU HERE FOR WORK TOMORROW, KOBATO-CHAN!
YES, MA'AM!

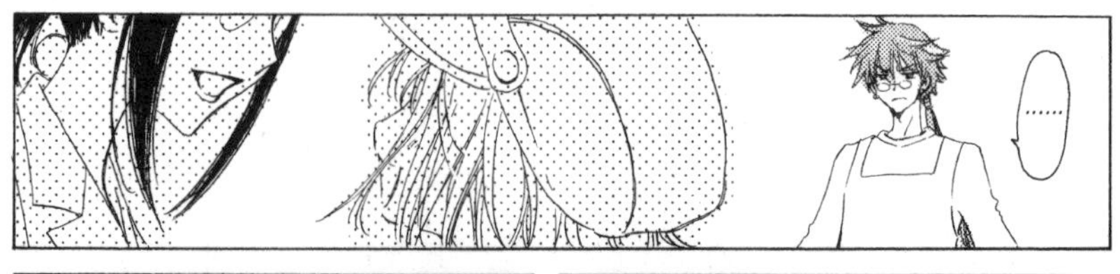
......

SU (PASS)
JUST REMEMBER! I DON'T APPROVE OF YOU!
むっかーっ
MUKAAA (GRRR)

MUNYA (MMM)
BRING ME ONE ORDER OF PIG'S FEEEEET!
MUNYA
I FINALLY FOUND A PERSON WHO WILL LET ME HEAL HER!
I'LL HAVE TO DO MY BEST!

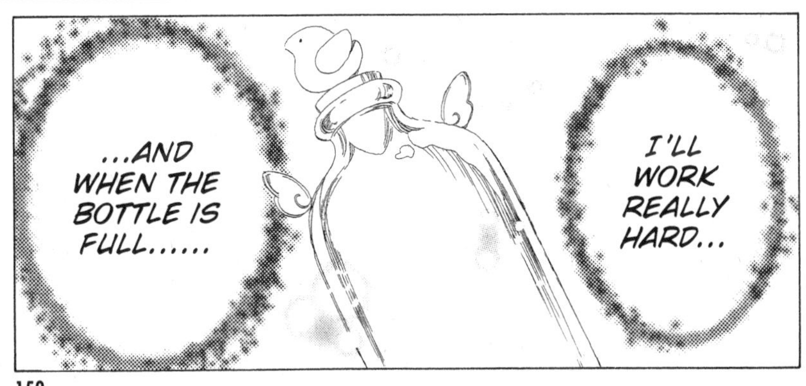
I'LL WORK REALLY HARD...
...AND WHEN THE BOTTLE IS FULL......

...I'LL BE ABLE TO DO IT......
MM...
JUURGH...
JUURGH...

to be
continued

TRANSLATION NOTES

COMMON HONORIFICS

no honorific: Indicates familiarity or closeness; if used without permission or reason, addressing someone in this manner would constitute an insult.

***-san*:** The Japanese equivalent of Mr./Mrs./Miss. If a situation calls for politeness, this is the fail-safe honorific.

***-sama*:** Conveys great respect; may also indicate that the social status of the speaker is lower than that of the addressee.

***-kun*:** Used most often when referring to boys (though it can be applied to girls as well), this indicates affection or familiarity. Occasionally used by older men among their peers, but it may also be used by anyone referring to a person of lower standing.

***-chan*:** An affectionate honorific indicating familiarity used mostly in reference to girls; also used in reference to cute persons or animals of either gender.

Page 5 - **Kobato Hanato**
Her first (personal) name is Kobato, and her last (family) name is Hanato. The kanji for Kobato means "baby dove" and Hanato means "flower door."

Page 11 - **Crows**
Crows are garbage-eating pests in Japan. They know when garbage is thrown out and go in to feed. Some anti-crow strategies include only allowing people to throw away their trash the morning of the pickup, nets to cover the garbage, and other measures, but the problem persists.

Page 13 - **Dobato**
Adding *do* to a Japanese word has a similar effect as that of adding a curse word to another word in English. For example, calling someone *aho* ("idiot") is insulting in its own right but still fairly tame. Calling someone a *doaho*, however, would be equivalent to saying "you're a (bleep)-ing idiot." Also, the literal meaning of Kobato's name brings to mind baby dove chicks, whereas "Dobato" is also actually an ornithological name that refers to feral pigeons and thus conjures up the idea of dirty pigeons that are a nuisance on the streets. So what's for certain is that Kobato is cute and Dobato definitely isn't.

Page 15 - ***Nabe***
Nabe, which literally means "cooking pot," is the name of a popular hot winter dish in Japan. When one says *nabe*, one generally thinks of meats and veggies boiled in an earthenware cooking pot from which the contents are taken, dipped in a small sauce bowl, and eaten. There are an infinite number of variations when it comes to cooking *nabe*.

Page 17 - **Spell**
In the Japanese version, Kobato is referring to the kanji that make up the word for "common sense," *joushiki*. Every kanji has its own way of being written (called stroke order), and for someone of Kobato's age to not know the proper stroke order for this word goes a little against common sense.

Page 17 - **Hokuto Shinken**
In the classic manga, *Hokuto no Ken* (*Fist of the North Star*), the main character Kenshiro is a master of the martial art Hokuto Shinken ("Divine Fist of the North Star"). Using it, he attacks with nothing but the ends of his index fingers, causing his enemies (as well as walls and asphalt) to be riddled with holes or even explode.

Page 18 - **Part-time-*kun***
In Japanese, not only names, but job titles can take honorifics.

Page 20 - ***Oden***
Like *nabe*, *oden* is another hot treat on cold Japanese days. *Oden* includes many signature items such as dumplings, fried tofu, large round slices of boiled daikon radish, seasoned hard-boiled eggs, etc. that are boiled in a water-based broth and served either on a plate, in a bowl, or skewered on a wooden stick.

Page 22 - ***Motsunabe***
A *nabe* (see above note) in which the main meat is tripe.

Page 24 - **Cook it for us**
Most *nabe* is cooked by the patrons (many having their own opinions on how it is best cooked), but having the waitstaff cook the *nabe* is not an unusual request.

Page 25 - *Natto*
A type of fermented soybean mixed in its own viscous juice. It can be put into such things as sandwiches and sushi, but it is not normally put into *nabe*.

Page 26 - **The bucket on the floor**
The arrow is pointing to a sick-bucket the food-stand owner brought just in case.

Page 30 - **Christmas Eve**
In Japan, Christmas is celebrated very differently than in the West. One difference is that it is mainly celebrated on the evening of December 24th.

Page 31 - **Spend the night in a hotel**
Another difference, and probably the biggest difference between Japanese and western celebration of Christmas is that in Japan, Christmas is mainly a date and/or party night. Many musicians hold Christmas Eve concerts, and other popular date spots are prebooked long in advance. Also, love hotels do a brisk business.

Page 33 - **Chitose**
Avid CLAMP readers may recognize the character designs of Chitose and her children from *Chobits*.

Page 33 - **Christmas cake**
Although the exact origin of the Japanese idea of Christmas cake is debatable, many believe it to be from France's tradition of *la bûche de Noël* ("Christmas log cake"). In any case, Japanese Christmas cake tends to be a lot like western birthday cake: round, sugary, and covered in tons of white frosting.

Page 34 - **Tirol**
This bakery has appeared in several CLAMP works before this such as *Chobits* and *Card Captor Sakura*. In keeping with Japanese trends for naming this type of store, the bakery's name most likely refers to the Austrian region of Tyrol (spelled "Tirol" in Austrian) that includes the city of Innsbruck. The characteristic architecture of the region seems to play into the shop's architecture and image, and so, it seemed the best translation for the shop name.

Page 87 - **Kobato-*kun***
Ioryogi's use of the honorific *-kun* makes him sound more like a teacher or superior of some kind. Since he usually uses her name without honorifics, it's something of a warning sign of his anger.

Page 87 - **Ainu dwarf**
The Ainu (Japan's aboriginal race that mostly live on the northern island of Hokkaido) have tales of a little people called Korobokkuru (or Koro-pok-guru, among other spellings) who dwelt under butterbur (*koro*) leaves. In many paintings and other depictions, these little people use the leaves as umbrellas. The Ainu believe that the Korobokkuru lived on the Hokkaido island before they came, and there is some disputed evidence that the folk tale may have some truth to it.

Page 93 - **Hot Station**
An advertising campaign for the Lawson chain of Japanese convenience stores claimed that their stores were "Your Town's Hot Station."

Page 95 - CLAMP fans might recognize the two main characters from *Suki Dakara Suki* in this scene.

Page 100 - ***Miiin-jiri***
Although cicadas aren't exclusive to Japan, they are so prevalent during the months of July and August that their sounds become shorthand to indicate the hottest part of the Japanese summer.

Page 104 - **Cool Biz**
The standard Japanese business suit worn during the hot, humid Japanese summer means that office air conditioning has to be cranked up, thereby wasting energy and money and adding to carbon pollution. In 2005, the government instituted the "Cool Biz" policy where government workers were encouraged (in some cases, required) to wear short-sleeve shirts and go without their suit coats and ties. And all offices were set to twenty-eight degrees Celsius (about 82°F).

Page 107 - **Ginsei**
The pronunciation for Ginsei starts with a hard "g" sound as in "get." It would then be pronounced "Geen-say."

Page 115 - **Give-away girls**
Look for characters from *Angelic Layer* and *Magic Knight Rayearth* in this scene!

Page 145 - **Extortion racket**
Called *tsutsumotase* in Japanese, it's a classic scam where a pretty young woman goes up to a man and propositions him for sex (paid or free), then in the hotel room or other private place, her "boyfriend," a gangster-type, bursts in and threatens the man for what he "did" to the gangster's girlfriend. Usually large sums of money are the only way to satisfy the gangster.

Page 147 - ***Enkou* and *uri***
Enkou is short for *enjou kousai*. Girls of high-school age or even younger arrange for dates with older men in return for money or expensive presents. The date does not necessarily have to result in sex, but the general expectation is that it will. *Uri* is Japanese slang for "prostitution." Both *enjou kousai* and *uri* are illegal.

Page 43 - ***Otoshidama***
Otoshidama is traditionally a gift of money at New Year's from parents and other adults to children.

Page 45 - **Quiet on New Year's**
In Japan, New Year's Day is for time spent quietly with family—the opposite of the western tradition. On New Year's, the Japanese get a couple of days off before and quite a few days off after New Year's Day so they can visit family in other parts of the country or spend the holidays at home. Although some shops do business on New Year's, most stay shuttered until some time after January 3rd.

Page 50 - **Elderly woman**
Some may recognize the elderly woman in this scene from her appearances in *xxxHOLiC*.

Page 52 - **Japanese New Year's**
This page displays a range of games and pastimes that are traditions on New Year's in Japan. Games such as the special version of battledore and shuttlecock and the card game *karuta* are often highlights of New Year's celebrations in Japan.

Page 54 - ***Mochi***
Mochi is rice that is beaten into a paste. It is a very popular dish in Japan and can be served in a wide variety of ways, such as baked, cooked in a soup, or served in a bowl with sweetbeans. The *otoshidama* mochi that the elderly fortune teller gives Kobato is probably a confection with *mochi* on the outside and a sweet bean paste filling inside.

Page 57 - **Valentine's Day**
In Japan, Valentine's Day is a day when women give chocolate to men. (Men have their chance to give in return exactly one month later on "White Day.") Although it's conceived as a day for lovers, gifts between workers, or from teachers to students, etc. also are popular.

Page 63 - ***Tsukkomi* and *boke***
Manzai is the name of the traditional Japanese two-man stand-up comedy act. In it, one comedian plays the *boke* or dumb guy, and the other plays the *tsukkomi* or angry guy. It plays out a little like Laurel and Hardy with the *boke* saying something absurd, and the *tsukkomi* coming back to complain at how stupid what the *boke* said was. Although Kobato isn't quite a typical *boke*, Ioryogi's reactions are very typical of a *tsukkomi*.

Page 71 - ***Ohanami***
Hanami (the "o" is simply an honorific) means, quite literally, "seeing/viewing flowers." In this case, the word refers to flower viewing parties for sakura cherry trees, the most viewed flower in Japan. Many parks, such as Ueno Park in Tokyo, are famous for their cherry trees and for flower viewing parties during the approximately two weeks of spring when the flowers bloom. The parks fill up quickly, so it's best to find a spot early and hold it. Flower viewing parties have a long tradition in Japan, and many customs, including those mentioned in this chapter, have been built up around them.

Page 85 - **Rainy day**
June is traditionally the rainy season in Japan. It's a time when it rains nearly every day, and those cheap, see-through-plastic umbrellas get a lot of use.

KOBATO. ❶

CLAMP

Translation: William Flanagan • Lettering: Alexis Eckerman

Edited by KADOKAWA SHOTEN
First published in Japan in 2007 by KADOKAWA CORPORATION, Tokyo. English translation rights arranged with KADOKAWA CORPORATION, Tokyo, through TUTTLE-MORI AGENCY, INC., Tokyo.

Yen Press
1290 Avenue of the Americas
New York, NY 10104

Visit us at yenpress.com
facebook.com/yenpress
twitter.com/yenpress
yenpress.tumblr.com
instagram.com/yenpress

First Yen Press Edition: May 2010

ISBN: 978-0-316-08536-6 (paperback)

10 9 8 7 6 5 4 3

OPM

Printed in the United States of America